LI

Edited by
Geoff Tibballs

CARLTON
BOOKS

First published by Carlton Books, 2002
In association with Granada Commercial Ventures
Copyright © Carlton Books, Ltd, 2002
Liverpool logo and crest ™ and © Liverpool Football Club &
Athletic Grounds PLC
Licensed by Granada Commercial Ventures

A CIP catalogue record for this book is available from the
British Library.

ISBN 1 84222 516 2

Printed in Singapore
2 4 6 8 10 9 7 5 3 1

INTRODUCTION

Bill Shankly, Tommy Smith, the Kop – the history of
Liverpool Football Club is rich in colourful characters
who have never been short of a sharp one-liner. You
only have to look at the number of ex-Liverpool
players who have become TV pundits. To think, Alan
Hansen was criticised by his former manager for not
having enough to say for himself!

Alongside the shafts of Scouse and Scottish wit, this
book contains more serious quotes offering rare
insights into the private lives and careers of the
players and management staff who have graced
Anfield. So if you want to know who Michael Owen
wants to be as big as or what Paul Ince rates better
than sex, read on.

' Shankly gave the players and the city their pride and passion back. If you didn't have the pride and the passion, then you didn't play for Shankly and you didn't play for Liverpool. '

Fan Ricky Tomlinson

LIVERPOOL
FOOTBALL CLUB

" When you have a Liverpool
shirt on your back as part of
the squad, you will do anything
to make sure you preserve
what it stands for. "

Gérard Houllier

❝ I've been on this planet for 45 years, and have supported Liverpool for 42 of them. **❞**

Roy Evans, *becoming manager in 1994*

"There are two great teams
in Liverpool: Liverpool and
Liverpool Reserves. "

Bill Shankly

' Three-one in your Cup final. **'**

*Victorious **Liverpool fans'** chant to
Everton following the 3–1 win at Goodison
in September 2001*

' For those of you watching in black and white, Liverpool are the team with the ball. '

Liverpool fans' *joke before the 1984 Milk Cup final with Everton*

If Everton were playing at
the bottom of my garden,
I'd draw the curtains.

Bill Shankly

‘ Don't worry, Alan. You'll be playing near a great side. ’

Bill Shankly *to Alan Ball after he joined Everton*

❝ I know this is a sad occasion but I think that Dixie would be amazed to know that even in death he could draw a bigger crowd than Everton can on a Saturday afternoon. ❞

Bill Shankly *at Dixie Dean's funeral*

Every time I come to this place (Anfield) I think, "This is brilliant, I'm playing for Liverpool."

Nick Barmby

"Some friends asked: "Why are you moving to Liverpool when you play for Bayern Munich?" Now they realise it was a great opportunity. "

Markus Babbel

❝ From my first day at Melwood,
I appreciated Liverpool's
special DNA. ❞

John Barnes

❝ I remember as a new boy looking forward to my first Friday team meeting with some anticipation, so imagine my surprise when Tommy Smith sat down a few chairs away, put his feet up and unfolded his copy of the *Sporting Life*. I was waiting for the sparks to fly but no, Bob just got on with his chat and left Smithy to get on with picking the next day's winners. ❞

Phil Neal

"The Kop was the best place in the world to watch football as you were surrounded by so many characters and passionate people. There used to be a bloke called "the Mad Brickie" who kept us all entertained by getting on the pitch at half-time."

Ricky Tomlinson

❝ The Kop's exclusive, an institution, and if you're a member of the Kop you feel you're a member of a society, you've got thousands of friends around you and they're united and loyal. ❞

Bill Shankly

❝ That first night was the greatest.
We were in the front row of the
Kemlyn stand. The whole time my
eyes were fixed on the Kop.
I couldn't believe it.
I was mesmerised. The steam
was rising and the noise
was incredible. ❞

Phil Thompson *remembering
his first visit to Anfield at the age of 11*

'The whole of my life, what they wanted was honesty. They were not so concerned with cultured football, but with triers who gave one hundred per cent.'

Bob Paisley *on the Kop*

‘The fans here are the greatest
in the land. They know the game
and they know what they want
to see. The people on the Kop
make you feel great yet humble.’

Bill Shankly

❝ I'm a people's man only
the people matter. ❞

Bill Shankly

YOU'LL NEVER WALK ALONE

LIVERPOOL
FOOTBALL CLUB

EST·1892

' When the ball's down the Kop
end, they frighten the ball.
Sometimes they suck it into the
back of the net. '

Bill Shankly

LIVERPOOL
FOOTBALL CLUB

❝ I would just love to have gone
and stood in the Kop. ❞

Kenny Dalglish

'You had to be strong to be on the Kop. When I was about 13, I tried to go in the middle where all the excitement was and almost got cut in half. I was only 5ft 7in. A big docker pushed the crowd back and I ducked out and went back to my usual place to the left of the goal. '

Elvis Costello

' There's no noise like the Anfield
noise and I love it! **'**

Ian St John

❛ This record sums up our spirit on the field. No player in my team struggles or battles alone. There's always someone there to help him. ❜

Bill Shankly *discussing 'You'll Never Walk Alone'*

‘ The highlight of the game was not our two goals or the three points we won. It was when our fans made the Kop sing "You'll Never Walk Alone". It was as if they couldn't come here and go home without hearing it sung in all its glory. It was very emotional, and something I'll remember forever. ’

Kevin Keegan *after Newcastle's 2–0 win at Anfield, 1994*

' Mind, I've been here during the bad times too. One year we came second. **'**

Bob Paisley

‘ There's Man United and Man City
at the bottom of Division One.
And by God they'll take
some shifting. ’

Bill Shankly *looking at the League table
early in the 1972/3 season*

"I remember Jimmy Adamson crowing after Burnley had beaten us that his players were in a different league. At the end of the season they were."

Bob Paisley

❝ Sometimes if you spit up in the air, it can come back in your face. ❞

Gérard Houllier *reacting to jibes from Crystal Palace's Clinton Morrison after the first leg of the 2001 Worthington Cup semi-final*

❛ I was the best manager in Britain because I was never devious or cheated anyone. I'd break my wife's legs if I played against her, but I'd never cheat her. ❜

Bill Shankly

❝ He was only an ordinary sized man, but he just had this presence, he used to stand so tall. When he stood in front of the Kop he had thousands in the palms of his hands. ❞

Ricky Tomlinson *in praise of Bill Shankly*

❛ Bill Shankly is as firm
as his handshake and that's
a real finger-crusher. ❜

Ron Yeats

❛ They say he's tough, he's hard, he's ruthless. Rubbish, he's got a heart of gold, he loves the game, he loves his fans, he loves his players. He's like an old collie dog, he doesn't like hurting his sheep. He'll drive them. Certainly. But bite them, never. ❜

Joe Mercer *on Bill Shankly*

If Bill had one failing, it was the fact that he did not like to upset players that had done so well for him. He was a softie at heart.

Bob Paisley

‘ One of my great regrets is that I got the chance to speak to Bill Shankly only the once. After I signed for Liverpool, John Toshack took me to Shanks' house to meet him. He gave me two pieces of advice: don't over-eat and don't lose your accent. ’

Kenny Dalglish

❝ I love challenges. I like the aggravation that goes with football management. **❞**

Graeme Souness *taking over at Anfield, 1991*

‘ Liverpool Football Club is all
about winning things and being
a source of pride to our fans.
It has no other purpose. ’

*Chairman **David Moores** dismissing
Graeme Souness as manager*

❝ I daren't play in a five-a-side
at Liverpool, because if I
collapsed, no one would
give me the kiss of life! **❞**

Graeme Souness *as his popularity waned*

❝Are we talking about a
change of religion here or just
a change of football club?**❞**

Gérard Houllier *over fears that Nick Barmby
may have had to go into hiding following his
move across Stanley Park*

'The people who come to watch us play, who love the team and regard it as part of their lives, would never appreciate Liverpool having a huge balance in the bank. They want every asset we possess to be wearing a red shirt.'

Kenny Dalglish

"It's there to remind our lads who they're playing for, and to remind the opposition who they're playing against."

Bill Shankly *explaining the significance of the 'This Is Anfield' plaque*

‘ When I went to see the chairman
to tell him, it was like walking
to the electric chair. ’

Bill Shankly *on his decision to quit*

❝ I had to say I was retiring, though I believe you retire when you're in a coffin and the lid is nailed down and your name is on it. **❞**

Bill Shankly

Some people believe football is a matter of life and death. I am very disappointed with that attitude. I can assure you it is much more important than that.

Bill Shankly

❝ I have only felt like this once before, and that was when my father died, because Bill was like a second father to me. ❞

Kevin Keegan *hearing of Bill Shankly's death*

When Bob appeared on television the public saw this guy with the wide grin on his face and that quaint Geordie accent which I could never really understand. He was like everybody's favourite uncle. But there was a completely ruthless streak in Bob. If he decided that a player had to be axed, then that was that. Sentiment did not come into it.

Alan Hansen

‘I spent the first year on a
good horse, but I was like
an apprentice riding the Derby
favourite. I was cautious and
went too wide round the bends.
We should have won
the Championship. ’

Bob Paisley

LIVERPOOL
FOOTBALL CLUB

YOU'LL NEVER WALK ALONE

EST. 1892

' He was a great man.
His motivation
could move mountains. **'**

Ron Yeats's tribute to Bill Shankly

❛ Bill Shankly set such a high standard. Liverpool have been geared to this sort of thing for 15 years. I have just helped things along. ❜

Bob Paisley, *winning his first title*

‟ He's broken that silly myth that nice guys don't win anything. „

Brian Clough *assessing Bob Paisley's triumphs*

❛ He, Joe Fagan and Ronnie Moran give the club that homely appearance, but beneath what might seem a soft exterior there is a hard centre. ❜

Jimmy Armfield *considering Bob Paisley's inner steel*

" I never wanted the job in the first place. "

Bob Paisley

❝ I'm too old and tired. It's a job for a young man's brains and energy. It's not an eight-hours-a-day-job, it's twenty-four hours a day. And there's no way you can get away from that. ❞

64-year-old **Joe Fagan** *stepping down as manager*

‘ Management is a seven-days-a-week job. The intensity of it takes its toll on your health. Some people want to go on for ever, and I obviously don't. **’**

Kenny Dalglish, *1991*

❝ The chief executive, Peter Robinson, and I had just sat down at our fortnightly meeting with the manager when he came out and said he wanted to finish. I jokingly said "This afternoon?" and he said "Yes". ❞

*Liverpool chairman **Noel White** reeling from Kenny Dalglish's shock departure*

❝ It's the equivalent to being with the prettiest woman in the world and only sleeping with her once a month. I prefer to sleep with someone slightly less pretty every night! ❞

Gérard Houllier's way of saying he didn't want the England job

❝ It's like any relationship. Sometimes it goes wrong and you simply have to work at putting it right again. There's no point trying to pretend it's perfect all the time. We don't sit here holding hands seven days a week. ❞

Roy Evans *on his partnership with Gérard Houllier*

❮ It wasn't her wedding anniversary, it was her birthday, because there's no way I'd have got married in the football season. And it wasn't Rochdale. It was Rochdale Reserves. ❯

Bill Shankly *refuting stories that he had taken his wife Nessie to watch Rochdale on their wedding anniversary*

❝ Liverpool had dug its claws
ever deeper into our psyche
until, at all times, the craving
to be simply the best lay
just below the surface. **❞**

Alan Edge
Faith of our Fathers

LIVERPOOL
FOOTBALL CLUB

YOU'LL NEVER WALK ALONE

EST·1892

Some people might think we are lazy, but that's fine. What's the point of tearing players to pieces in the first few days? We never bothered with sand dunes and hills and roads; we trained on grass, where football is played.

Bill Shankly *on pre-season training*

❛ I hate training, I hate running, but at Liverpool they say: if you don't put it in at training, how do you expect to put it in during a match? **❜**

Robbie Fowler, *1996*

LIVERPOOL
FOOTBALL CLUB

EST·1892

' To be the best you have
to forget the partying and
concentrate all your energies
on the football. '

Michael Owen

' We knew that all other things being equal, like skill, tactics and run of the ball, it was fitness that would count in the end. So we kept at 100 per cent at all times, and it paid us. We have found that there is more satisfaction in a good win than there is in a pint or a cigarette packet. **'**

Roger Hunt

'There used to be a drinking culture in football and I know because I was part of it.'

John Aldridge

❝ He's a walking advert for the benefits of junk food. He'll eat five packets of crisps and wash it down with Coke and Mars bars. ❞

Mark Lawrenson *weighs up Steve Nicol's diet*

❛ Young Gerrard has the world at his feet. For that age, he's some player, but even now, he could go anywhere, do anything. ❜

Bobby Robson

Steven Gerrard is Souness
with pace and that's
a hell of a player.

Alan Hansen

*If you ask any of the lads,
I think I can have a laugh just
like any other 20-year-old.
But at certain times I think
you've got to be serious and
have your head screwed on.*

Michael Owen

❝If he stays out of night
clubs for the next few years,
he can buy one.❞

Gérard Houllier *predicting a glorious future
for Steven Gerrard*

There was this little guy in midfield, lean and aggressive, yap, yap, yap on at others, boys older than him. I like that kind. I said: "He comes to me." They said: "No, not him, he has too many problems, with his back, with his muscles." But we worked with him.

Gérard Houllier *spotting Steven Gerrard*

❝ I grew up on a council estate.
We had a car park outside the
house and we put a goal up at one
end of it and played every second
we could. A lot of my mates there
are unemployed now so I do
think about what I might have
been doing without football. ❞

Steven Gerrard

Robbie Fowler's from the South End of Liverpool, like myself. People from that part of the world need to be tough to survive and make a name for themselves. And believe me, Robbie is tough.

John Aldridge

❝ He was like a fox in that area,
the way he hunted for his goals. ❞

Gérard Houllier *after Robbie Fowler's*
hat-trick against Aston Villa in 1998

'Who can say what he's going to do? It's a talent and you can't teach it, you can't coach it. All you can do is enjoy it.'

Roy Evans *discussing a young Robbie Fowler*

❛ God's job's a good 'un ❜

A **Robbie Fowler** *T-shirt to celebrate a goal*

Strikers are selfish, at least the very best are. It's not about giving everyone else a chance as far as you are concerned. You want to be out there on the pitch scoring goals. It proves you are a winner.

Ian Rush

❛ The thing about Michael is that he is fast, if defenders lose him for a moment they can't recover. Once Michael goes, they never catch him. On top of that is his finishing. He is so cold, even colder than a Swede. **❜**

*England boss **Sven-Goran Eriksson** drooling over Michael Owen*

YOU'LL NEVER WALK ALONE
LIVERPOOL
FOOTBALL CLUB
EST·1892

" He is the target for all
the hitmen in the game.
He is the man they are after,
yet few of them can kick
him out of the game. "

Bob Paisley *on Kenny Dalglish*

' I have never played with anyone as quick as him. It frightens everyone. Defenders back off when he gets the ball because they can't deal with it. It is great for me because you can hit a bad ball and the next thing, he is on to it and it is a great pass. '

Jamie Redknapp *admiring the pace of Michael Owen*

❝ He's just stepped out of the shower. Come in and see him…have a walk round him. He's a colossus. ❞

Bill Shankly *unveiling 6ft 2in, 14-stone centre-half Ron Yeats to journalists*

Sometimes you look at
a defender and think, yeah,
he's a big lad. But when I see
a big defender I think, great,
he can't turn.

Michael Owen

'With him at centre-half, we could play Arthur Askey in goal!'

Bill Shankly *on Ron Yeats*

‟ It's not nice going to the supermarket and the woman at the till thinking, "Dodgy keeper". „

David James *on his loss of form in 1997*

'The White Pelé? You're more like the White Nellie!'

Bill Shankly *as Peter Thompson struggled to reproduce his international form in Brazil on the domestic stage*

❛ He was struggling…he was probably too unselfish at the time. That's often the case with a young player, particularly one coming into a successful side. He tended to look for others and lay the ball off when he could have had a go himself. I told him to be a bit more selfish, and it wasn't long before the penny dropped. ❜

Bob Paisley *recalling Ian Rush's goal drought when he first arrived at Anfield*

❛ I realise now that computer games have affected my performance badly. The last time I had a nightmare was at Middlesbrough in the Coca-Cola Cup and I had played Nintendo for eight hours beforehand. ❜

David James

❝ People don't realise that getting married which Robbie did in the summer and becoming a family man can affect you. It's a hell of a transition which can have dramatic consequences. I remember Bob Paisley used to say you would have to forget players for up to 12 months if they had just got married and had children. ❞

Ian Rush

❮ You've got to treat every game as if it might be your last. Before you have a bad injury you don't think like that, but then you realise that people's careers do get ended. You think, "It could happen to me." Look at Rob Jones; he got a knee injury and never really played again. ❯

Robbie Fowler

❝ I find out more about a player
when he's injured. However
much you try to involve him,
he seems an outcast. You see
the reaction, the character
when a player is down. ❞

Bob Paisley

❝ It's a bit like the weather.
You know it is going to rain at
some stage but there is nothing
you can do to stop it.
It is just a matter of when. **❞**

Gérard Houllier *talking about Michael Owen's*
recurring hamstring problems in 2001

❝ Take that poof bandage off, and what do you mean you've hurt your knee? It's Liverpool's knee! ❞

Bill Shankly *to an injured Tommy Smith*

" When you see Tommy Smith
go down, then you know
he's been hurt. "

Bob Paisley

❝ Bottle is a quality too, you know.
It's not just about ball control
and being clever. Sometimes
you have to show the world
what's between your legs. **❞**

Graeme Souness

❝ We do things together.
I'd walk into the toughest
dockside pub in the world with
this lot because you know that
if things got tough, nobody
would "bottle" it and scoot off. ❞

Emlyn Hughes *on his Liverpool team-mates*

LIVERPOOL
FOOTBALL CLUB

YOU'LL NEVER WALK ALONE

EST·1892

"Tommy Smith would start a riot in a graveyard."

Bill Shankly

❝I love tackling. It's better than sex. A great tackle gets everybody pumped up. **❞**

Paul Ince

> 'He's got a baby face when he plays football, but when he tackles he knows what he's doing. '

Aston Villa boss **John Gregory** *on Michael Owen*

❝ My favourite player in the whole world is Michael Owen. **❞**

Pelé

❝ He is the best player that Liverpool have signed this century. It was the best decision we have ever made. He sets such a fine example, not just to our players but to everybody in the game. ❞

*Chairman **John Smith** praising Kenny Dalglish as Liverpool clinch the League title in 1986*

‘ The bottom line is that
Beardsley comes from God. ’

*Scotland chief **Andy Roxburgh** after Peter
Beardsley's winner for England in 1988*

❛ Don't you recognise him?
This man is the future
captain of England. **❜**

Bill Shankly *to a traffic policeman who had
stopped him on his way back to Liverpool
with new signing, Emlyn Hughes*

❝ I never saw anyone in this country to touch him. I can think of only two who could go ahead of him – Pelé and possibly Cruyff. ❞

Graeme Souness *on Kenny Dalglish*

❛ Kenny Dalglish was the reason
I signed for Liverpool. It was his
reputation and his stature in the game
that persuaded me and the fact that
he gave me a particularly smart pair
of boots. It is the only "bung" I have
ever received. They were two sizes
too big for me, but I didn't half
look good in them. ❜

Steve McManaman

❝ We got him from Home Farm,
the boys' club in Dublin, and
I think the lads who come to you
from that sort of background in
the game are the best type.
You get England schoolboys and
their heads are away before they
arrive at the club. I think the
failure rate is about 96 per cent. ❞

Bob Paisley *announcing the arrival of
Ronnie Whelan*

❝ Keegan has a Doncaster
childhood and a Scunthorpe
upbringing, yet he seems
to have been born with
Liverpool in his soul. ❞

Joe Mercer

❝ He was never the most gifted player, but I've never known anyone work so hard at his game. He made himself great. **❞**

John Toshack *on Kevin Keegan*

❝ If we had to lose our record, I'd sooner it be against Liverpool than anyone else. ❞

*Newcastle boss **Kevin Keegan** as Liverpool became the first team that season to take a point at St James' Park, 1994*

' Yes, he misses a few.
But he gets in the right
place to miss them. '

Bill Shankly *on Roger Hunt*

❝ Reputations do not mean anything to me. If they did, I would choose Ian Rush and Roger Hunt up front. ❞

Gérard Houllier

❝ Our goalkeeping coach, Joe
Corrigan, has done a fantastic
job on David's mental side.
Though you'll never get that part
completely right, because all
keepers are mental anyway. ❞

Roy Evans *on David James*

I'm not Superman. When you
are doing really well, people
go over the top and really
praise you. You don't complain
then, so why complain when
people have a go?

Michael Owen

❝ Footballers are recognised everywhere we go. We were in Dublin once, just doing a bit of shopping, and were mobbed in the street. It was like a scene out of a Beatles movie; we had to run to jump into a cab to escape. Another time I was even recognised on the Great Wall of China! **❞**

Steve McManaman

❝ I didn't realise it was going to be this high profile when I was out in France. It was only when I came back and got a great reception at the airport and then got home to find reporters camped on my doorstep that I realised what was happening. Even the away fans have been applauding me so far this season, which has been incredible. ❞

Michael Owen *after the 1998 World Cup*

❝ McManaman was a very deceptive player and to see him move on the field you wouldn't think he was travelling as fast as he was. It was only when you saw him outstrip people that you realised how fast he was. **❞**

Eric Sutcliffe, *former Secretary of the Liverpool Schools FA*

‘ Now, boys, Crerand's deceptive
he's slower than you think. ’

Bill Shankly preparing for a meeting with
Paddy Crerand and Manchester United

❝ We always had to win,
even friendlies. ❞

Tommy Smith

❝ Anybody who plays for me
should be a bad loser. ❞

Graeme Souness

❝ When we lose, it knocks me for six. I bring it home with me. It upsets my whole week. If you win on Saturday, you can't wait to go in on Monday because everybody will be buzzing but when you get beat, it is awful. **❞**

Jamie Redknapp

❝ I've never felt so bad in my life.
I let so many people down the
people of Liverpool, who I love. **❞**

John Aldridge *following his crucial
penalty miss in the 1988 FA Cup Final
against Wimbledon*

❝ I was really confident. I took a penalty in training and put it in the same spot. Just like that. ❞

Alan Kennedy *after scoring the winning penalty in the European Cup Final shoot-out against Roma in 1984*

❝ I have never been so nervous
in my life as when I ran on
to take that penalty. **❞**

John Aldridge *coming on as a sub to take a
penalty to put Liverpool 6–0 up against Crystal
Palace in 1989, his farewell match before his
move to Spain. Liverpool went on to win 9–0*

"Sure we get our share of penalties. But then we get in the penalty area more often than most teams."

Kenny Dalglish

Getting the Nou Camp booing their own players because they didn't touch the ball in the first ten minutes.

Emlyn Hughes *recalling his favourite moment from Liverpool's triumphant 1976 UEFA Cup run a semi-final trip to Barcelona*

"You get to wish that they would just occasionally pass the ball to the other team, like the rest of us do."

Watford boss **Graham Taylor** *despairing of playing Liverpool*

❝As the ball came over, I remembered what Graham Taylor said about my having no right foot, so I headed it in.❞

John Barnes *scoring against Taylor's Aston Villa in a 1988 FA Cup tie*

❝ The only way to beat Liverpool
is to let the ball down. **❞**

Portsmouth manager **Alan Ball**

❝ It's not about the long ball
or the short ball, it's about
the right ball. **❞**

Bob Paisley

' The Liverpool philosophy is simple, and is based on total belief. Maybe that has been the key to Liverpool's consistency. We were taught to go out there, play our own game and fear no one. **'**

Phil Neal

❛If I told people that the secret of Liverpool's success is a dip in the Mersey three times a week, I not only reckon they'd believe me but I think our river would be full of footballers from all over the country.❜

Club trainer **Ronnie Moran**

❝Our methods are so easy,
sometimes players don't
understand them at first.❞

Joe Fagan

❝ I always have my packet of chocolate buttons. **❞**

Peter Beardsley *explaining the secret of his success*

❝I want to build a team that's invincible, so they'll have to send a team from Mars to beat us.❞

Bill Shankly

'Even Ian Callaghan had to bend down to get through the door after one of Shankly's team talks. It was amazing how he could build you up.'

Ron Yeats

❝ We didn't know what he was talking about half the time but we knew what he wanted. ❞

Tommy Smith *trying to follow Bob Paisley's mangled English*

'Bob would call us together
on a Friday morning and usually
just say "The same team
as last week", and we
would get on with it. '

Mark Lawrenson

There's so many clubs been ruined by people's ego. The day after we won our first European Cup, we were back at this club at 9.45 in the morning, talking about how we would do it again, working from that moment, because nobody has the right to win anything they haven't earned.

Bob Paisley

'Anfield without European football is like a banquet without wine.**'**

Roy Evans

‘I don't know what will happen
when he goes full-time! ’

Bobby Robson *on Kenny Dalglish's success
as player/manager, 1988*

❝ What do I say to them in the dressing-room? Nothing really. Most of the time I don't even know what they are going to do myself. ❞

Kenny Dalglish

'We gave four great examples of how to score goals, and four bad examples of how to defend.'

Kenny Dalglish *after a 4–4 FA Cup tie with Everton in 1991*

❝ I know I may come over as a miserable git, but that was kamikaze defending. Managers would be dead within six months if every game was like that. ❞

Roy Evans *after a 4–3 win over Newcastle, 1996*

❝ Matt has got a bad back. I tell you it's two bad backs! And not much of a midfield either. ❞

Bill Shankly *putting the boot into United*

‘A good skipper, but he could have been a really great one if he had been a bit more extrovert.’

Bob Paisley *summing up Alan Hansen*

' Incey keeps you on your toes because he never stops moaning. **'**

Jamie Redknapp *about his former midfield partner Paul Ince*

'Tommy Smith wasn't born
he was quarried. '

David Coleman

❝ I was given the T-shirt by a friend of my dad's, who was one of the 500 dock-workers sacked. I thought I would wear it under my shirt, merely as a small statement of support. It is not politics. I am not trying to change people's opinions. It was essentially a fun thing. ❞

Steve McManaman *after he and Robbie Fowler wore T-shirts supporting the striking Liverpool dockers during a 1997 European tie with SK Brann of Norway*

❝ I swear that when we first
walked out onto the pitch
most people thought we
were the band! **❞**

Robbie Fowler *grimacing as he remembers
the cream suits worn on Cup Final day, 1996*

'Barnesy's chucked me a couple of cast-offs, things he hasn't worn or he never really liked. A few years ago he gave me a jacket covered in the Chinese alphabet. I love it but it's a bit loud.'

Barry Venison *assessing John Barnes's wardrobe*

‘ Some fruit and vegetable
dealers did very well. ’

John Barnes *after Everton fans hurled
bananas at him during a derby*

"I have a pair of old black laces that go everywhere with me. I don't wear them in my boots any more but I still use them to keep my socks up. If I ever lost them my career would be over."

Jason McAteer, *1995*

❝ It's nice to have a Paddy at the club again because the place never seems quite the same without an Irishman around. ❞

Roy Evans *signing Mark Kennedy*

‘ Dortmund will be very worried about Michael because they know just what he is capable of. Fortunately this time around he's on my side. ’

Dietmar Hamann *previewing a 2001/2 Champions' League match a few days after Michael Owen's hat-trick for England against Germany*

"I'd certainly like to be as, er, big as Lara Croft one day."

Michael Owen *at the launch of his own computer game*

'Chairman Mao has never seen such a show of red strength in all his life.'

Bill Shankly *addressing 300,000 fans as the 1974 FA Cup is paraded through the streets of Liverpool*

For far too long our fans have had to see a team in the backwaters of English football, so it is great to have people talking about Liverpool again.

Phil Thompson *celebrating the 2001 treble*

‘Liverpool was made for me
and I was made for Liverpool.’

Bill Shankly

' My philosophy is that the club is
more important than anyone! **'**

Gérard Houllier

"Are you Shankly in disguise?"

Fans singing to Gerard Houllier after the 2001 treble